WHISKEY BULLETS

0091

OTHER BOOKS BY
GARRY GOTTFRIEDSON

100 Years of Contact (Secwepemc
Cultural Education Society, 1990)

*In Honor of Our Grandmothers: Imprints
of Cultural Survival* (Theytus Books, 1994)

Glass Tepee (Thistledown Press, 2002)

Painted Pony (Partners in Publishing, 2005)

COWBOY AND INDIAN HERITAGE POEMS

Garry Gottfriedson

RONSDALE PRESS

WHISKEY BULLETS
Copyright © 2006 Garry Gottfriedson

RONSDALE PRESS
3350 West 21st Avenue
Vancouver, B.C., Canada V6S 1G7
www.ronsdalepress.com

Typesetting: Julie Cochrane, in New Baskerville 11 pt on 13.5
Cover Design: Julie Cochrane
Cover Art: William McAusland
Paper: Ancient Forest Friendly Rolland "Enviro" — 100% post-consumer
    waste, totally chlorine-free and acid-free

Ronsdale Press wishes to thank the Canada Council for the Arts, the Government of Canada through the Book Publishing Industry Development Program (BPIDP), and the Province of British Columbia through the British Columbia Arts Council for their support of its publishing program.

Library and Archives Canada Cataloguing in Publication

Gottfriedson, Garry, 1954–
    Whiskey bullets: cowboy and Indian heritage poems / Garry
Gottfriedson.

ISBN-13: 978-1-55380-043-9
ISBN-10: 1-55380-043-5

    I. Title.

PS8563.O8388W44 2006   C811'.6   C2006-903524-5

At Ronsdale Press we are committed to protecting the environment. To this end we are working with Markets Initiative (www.oldgrowthfree.com) and printers to phase out our use of paper produced from ancient forests. This book is one step towards that goal.

Printed in Canada by Hignell Printing

CONTENTS

Koyoti Indian

—

Copenhagen Cave

—

Whiskey Bullets

—

Shadow Walk

—

ACKNOWLEDGEMENTS

This book is written to honour two stimulating cultures, that of cowboys and Indians. I grew up in an exciting rodeo and ranching family, and I am a part of and love both the cowboy and Indian cultures. My blood brothers to whom I dedicate this book are great rodeo/ranching cowboys. And through my mother, I have learned the finer principles of my Indianness. I have the best of all worlds.

Also, I cannot forget about the bravery of other First Nations writers in Canada and the United States for their words of inspiration. The voice of my people has always been here, but only recently has it been taken seriously in Canada. And so, I acknowledge two brilliant writers to whom I turn when I am lost for words: Richard Van Camp and Joy Harjo. Thank you for your inspiration, wisdom, encouragement and friendship.

I wish to thank my family: my children, Vince and Storme, and also my grandchildren. It is because of you that I write, and some of the poems within this book offer glimpses of you.

A number of the poems in this collection have appeared in *Spirit Magazine* in 2005 and in previously published anthologies.

This book is dedicated to my brothers,
all of whom are cowboys and Indians.
For Bob, Ron, Frank, Ted, Oliver, Gus, Jr., and Guy.

It is also dedicated to my children
Storme & Vince
who gave me grandchildren
to carry on the legacy.

Koyoti Indian

Koyoti Indian

in perfect English, Koyoti commentaries stalk
TV cameras, recycled newspapers & the *National Inquirer*

during prime time news hour me and Koyoti
crack open lies over Labrador tea you know

old language does not die young
just as me & Koyoti are Indians from way back

we speak the same subtle dialect
spiritless tongues wagging in air

deep dark places & dirty sounds breaking
loose from the bed long past supper

fingers grip rhapsody
& the river ride begins the exchange of strawberries

evening gossip spreads
like high-tech trauma

the story cackles over breakfast eyes
speaks excitedly about last night's ebony skin & hard bone

me & Koyoti interject — turn on the tap, have a word about
ice-water . . . unbuttoned 501s . . . Players Light . . .

contentment known as sounds
breaking silence over twisted metaphors

meant getting screwed without first being kissed
blurted for a fortnight in perfect English

An Identity Crisis

I certainly know who I am . . .

I can get away with being politically incorrect.
I am the ambassador to First Nations' poetic expressions
& as Kinsella pompously put it straight
"I have the license to do so."

what a magical way to escape tyranny!
just like Trudeau & Chrétien hiding beneath cowboy hats

nevertheless & back to the point,

call me cowboy
call me First Nations
call me aboriginal
call me native
call me chug
call me skin

if you must,
but never call me Indian.
I call myself that!

& if you feel guilty when I say so,
this is not about postcolonial rhetoric
it is about an identity crisis

Bars

the well dried up at the Indian bar
a buck-fifty & a fat joint ago

in the old days, Indians stood outside
cowboy bars speaking to themselves

nobody listened
then or now

because lies are louder
than the measurement of sound

fighting beyond the bars is
a sub-culture norm, and

Indians have come to know that
resilience is the size of a fist

and broken spirits droop
necklaces of busted teeth along

the bunk house walls afterwards
outside they still piss beer

images of being sorry
when the last call is boomed

Tracks

crack & heroine love is free-based
like this free verse poem

the thrill only lasts
until the rubber band busts
or until the ink runs out

three hundred and sixty-five lies
is the creative approach
all cooked in a day's fix

your sorrow is good enough
until welfare Wednesday
and today is already Tuesday

next week you will beg me
with another set of bloodshot eyes,
tracks & broken needles

& all I will have to say is
cowboys and Indians don't pick quick-fixes

Saturday Night in Church

Saturday night in a creamy church
during cowboy mass filled
with carnations, Armani & Eau Sauvage
two men, one bald & the other sharing similar features
    with Jesus,
wore autumn crimsons, zebra colours and cowboy hats
they toasted Concha y Toro
to one & the other's sins.

The church had no pews
for the gaping audience
but there was a long line on both sides
marble confession boxes
where eager sinners waited
to confess churchgoer lies
before telling a gossiping midnight god
(who was also creamy).

The procession moved
to the balconies of God's bedroom
where organists played
Hank Williams' "How Great Thou Art"
while frenzied hummers swayed shoulder to shoulder
back to back, back to front, & belly to belly.

They believed in the song
dropping hats to the floor
& no one questioning it;
no one seemed to hit a bad note
or fall off key (even at 4:00 A.M.)
but by five, the choir stopped
& the mortal sinners & servants once more
toasted their visitors & then themselves
before they disbanded

in hope
to find a noon Sunday service.

Inspiration

Inspiration is the illusory cowboy enthusiast,
lazy emotions lying on a dormant saddle
blanket bed and weather-beaten saddle awaiting
a sexy sign to erect the sleepy ranch hand to scream

"I have to write something . . . anything . . .
senseless as it may be . . ."

frantic when the pen is dry
or the paper is drooping wet
with Patsy Cline tears
with spilled black coffee
with smudged country-and-western lines
that hold the subconscious thought

and ready for the scholars
to go . . . "hmmmm . . . this line, this writer, this poem
seems to contain sexual innuendoes"
when in fact there is no relationship
most of the time . . .

it is merely the moment
when the cattle-driver's love of writing
pours through the pen

and once again triumphantly thumps out
writer's block

Fly Spray

the Indian sees
a fly landing
on the dry meat rack turning
brown labour of carcass talk into
decomposition

Damn! Not again! he thinks,
skyscrapers of maggots taking over
Indian possessions

call it the "law of nature"
if you must

but remember
the cupboard is full of
Raid

Cowboy Hats

the cowboy hat might fool you . . .

in my barn, broaden your knowledge of the horse
your journey wheels of horsemanship

but never mind that, to say the least.
attempting a move along the barn wall develops principles

not necessarily in the right order, but what the hell!
feeling important is important, don't you agree?

the charger connection is the ladder that
leads to heaven . . . climb aboard

the ultimate expression of harmony . . . the foundation
to garner respect, gain control & achieve confidence . . .

electrifying means moving along
round penning skills identifies the horse action

crack the whip to begin the merry-go-round.
& discover the pony

rapidly responds to your hand stroke
at the sound of the explosion

Now where is that cowboy hat?

Caucasian Young Men Cattle Rounder-uppers (Cowboys) and First Nations (Indians)

young students, multicultured Canada, citizens of globalized continents, may I introduce cowboys and Indians? *oops,* I do apologize! I really am a polite politically corrected mixed race citizen of this great nation and mosaic of Canada, and a wonderful history teacher, really. please do allow me to re-try. children, may I introduce Caucasian Young Men Cattle Rounder-uppers and First Nations, along with half-breeds . . . *sorry! sorry!* I did mean those born of multicultural non-discriminating parents. I, myself, am of mixed race descendants . . . so you see, I have no ill bones whatsoever . . . now, to continue . . . the integration of both societies (one civilized, the other savage) created the world of rodeo, these two dynamic and fascinating paradigms have for the past two hundred years co-inhabited charmingly. their story begins on the wide open range of wind-swept prairie grass-lands with Koyoti (the legendary mythical First Nations figure) concocting magic. did I say Koyoti howled a fortnight? yes, the legends behold Koyoti howling holy hymns for the sole purpose of amalgamation. did I see a hand wagging for my attention? yes, that is correct . . . amalgamation . . . amalgamating of the two horny toads for both to fornicate then followed by the opposite of each sex birthing mixed blood offspring. this is also a sex-ed class. need I remind you. to continue. I have heard this from an esteemed elder. and so the narrative goes Caucasian Young Men Cattle Rounder-uppers and First Nations, along with their half-breed offspring, enjoyed friendly competition. rodeo was now born. they fucked . . . *oh no! I did it again.* I did mean they bucked horses as the breezes fluttered their hair wildly below the sun. they rode the wide open plains, bucking and galloping and fucking joyously. just like Tonto and the Lone Ranger, Sitting Bull and Custer, Sacagawea and awh . . . awh . . . the name has slipped me . . .

Oh, I do beg your forgiveness . . . I really am muddling up this righteous story . . . I must end it here . . . please resort to your dominant culture interpretive history texts for the rest of the lesson . . . thank you. you are dismissed.

Moral Principles

scientific methodology does
not necessarily mean
saving the environment

the Indian thinks about
the cowboy cowboying range land
and the scientist who doesn't
understand
destructive nature
or the natural law

a capitalist naturally at heart,
the theorist disguises foolishly
moral principles
concerned about bug kill
pine beetles
plastic

Indian and cowboy
ethics
relentlessly
honour their Mother

now, how does science
fit into that?

Bully

a pony-ride'n Indian gal once said
in the most sophisticated feminist tone

"punctuate moments of acute fear
and outline transparency. . . " (like an essay)

breathlessly and confidently she sported
pointy-toed cowboy boots
ribbon shirts
a whip-pouting femininity
but lashing from a fake Adam's apple

"conceptualize, if you will, the mental model of importance
(to hold hostage a predetermined prisoner)
and when you have done this"

she stopped abruptly to dig deep
then touted bull-whip sharp language

"preview the principles of independent, critical thinkers
and you may discover cultural disobedience —
which I hate". . . for I really am a bully

Trapped

Eyes that melt hate
in the corners where black pearls gouge
age lines hundreds of years old
along the rock face frozen in time

Hatred
petrified
where once glimmering gold fish flash-danced
in sea-speckled splendour

Crooked is a mouth
that has for centuries hissed
vile words mistaken
for love of its people & nation

The words used
never existed in my vocabulary
nor were snorted
through the nostrils
like a raging beast
firmly positioned
for the kill

Revulsion pulsing
at the edge of skin   redness trapped
in the turmoil   earthquake trembling
from the crown to the roots & back again
blocking every sound of reason, compassion & justice

Fists coiled
in the aftermath of contempt
charged with thousands of volts
of electrical rage waiting to give birth
to PEACE

Feminist's Thought

cowgirl on the other side — my other self
has advanced her whiskey-sharp words
directly towards my manly affairs
to argue, "touch thy womanly side"

but is it worth the release
of my masculine drive to fantasy?

I am man, through & through,
in love with my practical self,
analytical & Koyoti conniving
all the way to the football kickoff
between the upright posts, stiff & spread-
eagled on the player's bench
or ride'n wild bareback slide'n
spurs shoulder long until the knees
jerk delight

cowgirl, you tell me, "a womanly man needs to cry
freedom, instead of play in the National Football League
or ride at the Calgary Stampede"

but is it worth the release
of my masculine drive to fantasy?

I am man, through & through,
in love with my practical self,
analytical & Koyoti conniving,
I can never surrender
to lipstick & pantyhose & feminist thought
& if I cry, there will be no more man left
in me to enjoy sport or ride mares

Rocking Chair

the chair that rocks the ass hole
in the chief & council chambers
squeaks clean the rusty springs

supporting enchanted stories
that convince & convert colleagues
that truth is a fable
left for unseen generations to unravel

by then, no one will remember
what it means to be Secwepemc
& it will be left to future storytellers
to come clean with a different story

Secwepemc: a person from the Shuswap tribe

Political Questions

I had never thought
that cowboy & Indian intimacy was
a religious or political question
at least not until I met you

the story of who picked/s
the forbidden fruit
from the Garden of Eden
was a fairytale meant
to oppress the natural recourse

besides, was god so politically correct
that he/she would hold his/her
natural law in contempt?

you see, the snake
was only a seasoned politician,
a priest for political correctness,
& a fine used-car salesmen

there was no other
who had a cleaner belly than he/she

so let the cowboy & Indian be
who they are

& remember god was a virgin.

Anna Mae Aquash

feasts of white lies and charcoal tears drive
poetry to become dirty history lessons
but the story must be told

begin with Anna Mae Aquash;
MicMac woman warrior, 5'6", black hair, black eyes,
bullet in back of head, hands sliced off at wrists

There is more . . .

Custer fucked his way into the '80s.
rose from the grave,
disguised himself as FBI and CIA
raping Indian women
spraying bullets
hacking off hands,
filling Indian bodies with
lead sleeping in a man's dream

a finger print in the mind,
and blood payment
forever remembered

Victims

the theology of self-acclaimed power
cowboy or Indian excluded
is the perception of absolute identity
whirling like a rampant grassland fire
beneath that scalp of yours

it is the pretense
that you are all that could be
lower than the sun
but higher than everyone else

the indoctrination is the buy-in
for your theories are your truth
when in fact truth is a communal concept
both tribal and ranchland alike
that offers peace and liberation

the above has nothing
to do with belief systems
but everything to do with control
in the same way the rapist
conquers his/her victims

if you should lose your forsaken authority
or not have it to begin with,
influence or individuality
might mean — freedom

Backstabbing

this is not backstabbing
insists that bad back councillor
while moaning imaginary aches

huff & puff convincing pain
worthy enough for the mother chief

to write his speech before
she adjusts her elder's in-training bra
trying to alleviate the prick wedged between the clip
   & the spine

she covers up
her eternal stupidity, like a habit

Strep Throat

bad-mouthed Canadians
promised good-faith makers
land cramped by starvation sworn
a sack of flour, a cow, a treaty suit
exchange woodlands, prairie & mountains
for steep antagonism & acid love

charming was the speech
but too many spaces
between the teeth & tongue open
the tunnel to strep throat

& how could Koyoti
be sung back to life?

Sun Peak Lies

Koyoti caught
mouth drooping
saliva tongue dragging on
the sun-baked ground
heading west off Alpine Road
panting dry-throated
with his Stetson tilted
from the earth to the moon

Koyoti's desperate
attempts to straighten out
rattlesnake stories
coiling and smouldering
in land claims questions

"Just another cover up"
Secwepemc women sneer
vowing to sing
the Buffalo back to life
and make ready
the Medicine Calling Song

"Sure sounds good — all that harmony"
escapes Koyoti's thoughts
then Buffalo came
running to the rescue
and so did Wolverine
modelling
a red-neck ball cap

And now you know the rest of the story . . .

Koyoti Moon Story

like Koyoti
I toiled half-heartedly
across plains not sure
I could continue

staring into air
searching for the Moon's flip side
Koyoti promised to hide
things meant to be found

when I looked into your eyes
after the Sun went down
I thought I found you
but it was myself I saw

like a symbol
the Moon broke stride
and so a fresh creation story
(neither mine nor yours)
reminded Koyoti to sleep
with one eye open
because night is full of magic

inside the Moon's distance
Old Koyoti crooned for a young
man's magical form to awaken
hairline cracks in dreams visible
but on the other side remember
Koyoti can turn himself into anything
including words

Old Agendas

yesterday was January 1st
a cowboy & Indian get-together
time to clear out
last year's garbage

first the Indian binds useless agendas
in pink rubber bands & discards them
in Mr. Clean kitchen catchers
slumped by the back door,

next the cowboy retrieves paper scrap promises
that open the gate for midnight rodeo whispers
that will escape tomorrow
but today is already here

& Christmas is around the corner
wigwagging a fat man to
bring whiskey-bullet gifts
stacked 5-Star high

under the sparkling tree
the Indian smiles with crowned teeth,
You have to go, Babe.

so the cowboy packs
his rig & awaits the next Christmas rodeo

Copenhagen Cave

Copenhagen Cave

out of the darkness
near the morning light
excruciating pain
cables
his Copenhagen cave

pulsating electric fire
corroding every nerve
a cowboy takes
for granted

dignity is blood
turning to mercury

Yank the son-of-a-bitch out
he growls
clench-mouthed
with knuckle-white fists

and so it happens,
infectious poisons plaster
the dentist's plastic hands

Oh, relief! he sighs
one less tooth

A Week of Blindness

spurs are traps on the floor
boots are lead weights
pinning me to nowhere

my eyes gummed shut
dread to pry sickness
from the core's skylight

tears repel remediation
and the washcloth is somewhere else

I know now that
panic is god's verdict
and I have no control

I have learned
that blindness is to see
the world in a different perspective
forever taken for granted

A Cowboy's Ethics

a cowboy's work ethics
start at 5 A.M. with rest at 11 P.M.

there isn't always enough time
for wild rice, corn or deer meat

because the sun has its work cut out

since money grows from beneath
the hides of cows

cowboys never weaken,
they just grow thick skin

Collective Process

the collective process preached
was a sermon
left at the pithouse door
near Coyote Rock

death word composition
meant an Okanagan woman's prayer
was not collectiveness at all
instead, it was lethal destruction
decimating friendship
near Coyote Rock

Okanagan Fruit

it's a waste of time
sawing on the keyboard
in search of the perfect apple
when apples are perfectly cultivated
on the back porch
through cultural pressure

yet, it might've been
a redneck Indian that first shone
the gloss into the skin
but it was an Okanagan
who took the first bite

oh yes, the first snap is the finest
but just wait until you hit the core

Concocted

You're childless, so said the plastic scientists
but then, Red Stone and Willow ignited the Sky
rumbled a baby song

and you were on its path

Koyoti concocted magic, not just once, but twice,
Thunder clapped in your womb
to rattle an egg splitting into two

and so you became the life-giver,
I the receiver

now that is a miracle!

The Malaise of an Indian Woman Guru

the malaise of an Indian woman guru
dehydrated her heart in public
over the airwaves forever alive

the act was a scene
from the *Rez Sisters*
sending shivers through
the livewires buzzing
fruitful gossip of air-travel rape

but when the truth
spilled
turned
rebounded
all she could do was curl
into a 1940's fetal position

twice defeated

Tonto and the Lone Ranger

Cowboys and Indians alike brew
dangerous undercurrents
in the soul's skylight

cross-cultural stories steeping
icy compassion and sliver-sharp love affairs
never written in the Western Horseman, curriculum or poetry
because academic content is censored

Tonto and the Lone Ranger were never exposed
on prime time as fantasy in America or Canada
but the viewers drooled throbbing electrical currents
hallucinating reality tv

Prospect

the oldest Indian dance began
within the center of himself

it is where white stars create themselves
as other circles, brighter & smaller

travelling the prospect
of cowboy illusion

crawling across sky
in memory's landscape:

sweating Red paint & panting
the Blue Grouse Hop

once more the skin is full
of damp moss, autumn rain & heaven

No Names, Blank Faces

I've read poetry
to cowboys & Indians
with no names

blank faces
wanting to saddle me

ride bareback in rain
on cloudy days

imprints create puddles
vivid in memory tracks

I remember yesterday
in Regina

saddle bronc is a man's sport
played in the rain there

common players
common people

break & spill
in arenas of lined paper

surreal is poetry that lives
waiting for no names & blank faces

Masterpiece

dawn cracked the sky hours
death is one day younger
in the life of this cowboy & Indian

the clock's black & white hands
time-ticking invisible breaths
follow the Sun's trail

days & nights weave
another fiber
to be fed to the ever-so-patient
everlasting rest

food & drink, laughter & fear, love & hate
are victims

with jealousy the only friend of time
waiting in the red glow
of night

Standby

the reward for patience
is the "if" syndrome

possibilities overlap
time after time

when you climb
out of the saddle

or when you wait
for a flight out

faults do not exist
because connections were made

prior to the meeting
and when the horse is set

free
standby

Whiskey Bullets

Whiskey Bullets

I am in love alone
filling my mouth
with whiskey bullets

staring at upside down
carnations and lilies
hanging from ceiling corners
wishing they could resurrect
dead love

wilted flowers and whiskey bullets
are weapons and ugly realizations
that I will never
be good enough for you

Art

I am the cowboy artist
who gazes at Indian art

my eyes trace
passion imagined
on tepee walls

I dream of Indians

with pencil in mind
stories unfolding
on watercoloured paper
where truth is instinctive

I ponder roping
a painted Indian on canvas
but this has already been done

I am the cowboy artist
who gazes at Indian art

Journeys with Horsechild

in the Moon when the North Wind is here to stay
and you have completed your protective journey
from Koyoti rock to Koyoti Rock
and I from riding the Blizzard's snowflakes

tswentsu'temkuwc
towards the warmth of my lodge
giggling excitement
for what lies ahead will not be a mystery

me7 tkllentsu'tken enwi7
so that once again the mountains and ridges
the contours of your fire-lit body
will glisten wildly
as we ride towards dreamtime

---

tswentsu'emkuwc: we will gallop
me7 tkllentsu'tken enwi7: I will undress you

A Throat Song for Horsechild

in the Moon when your thunder hooves
descend to the bunchgrass
the sagebrush will part
to your dancing arrival
as you weave a Grass Dance
towards the hand drummers
chanting
with eyes closed
the Painted Horse Song

I will move my body
in rhythm to yours
and somewhere deep within my throat
I will sing you
into me
to become one —
Horsechild

Freckled Stars for Horsechild

In the Moon when the yellow jackets become dying arrows
the tips of birch leaves turn ochre
and will bend towards our Mother
offering their lives
to build anew in *sqepts*

I will gaze towards the Centre Pole
with the hand-drums ready
to vibrate the Lonely Heart Song

Wherever you are, Horsechild
face Deer Mountain and you will hear
the wind-swept songs sweeping
sweet harmony until the skies freckle with stars

Ready them carefully, my adored
for my story is waiting for you

Sqepts: summer

Blood-Telling Stories for Horsechild

in the Moon when our relatives are plump
and nearly ready for Winter
the geese in loud harmony
sky-dance along the path
that the Robins and Hummingbirds cleared beforehand

Horsechild, make your hand Crow-hop
along the taut skin of my belly
and you will feel my blood-telling stories

place your eager ear atop
my rumbling skin
and you will hear whispers
calling your name

allow your eyes to meet mine
and I will soul-pull you into me
for it is my turn to provide
you with a safe place — Horsechild

Icy Death

Twice you lifted the bottle
to your mouth and pulled the trigger.

Twice you escaped.

On the third, the river's raw power
spun a beckoning song.

You danced towards its vortex.
And this time, you jumped.

I saw your body like a crucifix
near the shore on an ice island
turning black from waist to toe.

And I reeled in your body
beneath a streetlight halo.

I lay my tingling skin on yours
praying you would escape
icy death.

Hot blood was the saviour.
Ice-burnt membrane thawed.

Then I set eyes on yours
weeping snowflakes
as I bargained with God
not to lose you a fourth time.

In your awakening
you called it luck.

I called it a miracle.

Cowboy Up

the "cowboy's code" is
mind your own business
never whine
never show pain
never allow the soul to scream
"I can't take it"
as you shank me dead on

when the code is broken
his death is more raw
than killing love

I am a pony-ride'n cowboy
black as it may be

thinking words
"cowboy up"
resistant
to Hollywood and reality tv

I've never used
my voice to utter
what lives within

and never forgotten
dad showed me
all the secrets to
being a cowboy

Apples

I have seen your wishy-washy love
at work beneath that cowboy hat and all

sleek and magnificent moving parts
slithering in and out of your wet
mouth and pearly teeth

your moon-red words are perfectly
round and precise like red delicious apples
ripe and ready country-and-western syllables
fall from the tree in Indian summer

Duck!

the rock is falling

Guitar Player

Where do you want my heart now?

Placed next to yours
on your pale skin
so that I will fall
in love with your sweaty pain

I have heard
your bones crack the dry cement
that leafed the frenzied spirit within

I witnessed its wildness escape into your body
screaming kissy words
while your fingers plucked at my guitar

your eyes were Koyoti's & Ska-lu-la's
trying to rip a path to my soul

& I froze there in my manly state
knowing there's nothing that I can do

Ska-lu-la: the monster

Electrical Currents

Indians want electrical currents,
bodies in approbation,
positive and negative fires screaming
death to dignity
in the story of fur and teeth
fingers belly dancing
where the current boils
blood to the edge of the skin

the disillusion is a sparking flame
nine years dead and desperate
ugly truth of unadulterated torches

is this good enough for a cowboy when
the wire is lying on the floor?

Cowboy Fire

cowboy fire dreams become obscured seconds
ebbed within chute-challenging aspirations

it is a double-beat dance,
blows and prowls of spurs
whizzing song
scraping hide
kicking air

under the skin the mind carves
courage when the chute gate pops
open to cheering crowds of wannabees
and buckle bunnies flipping hair air wide
wishing they could crawl into his dreams smouldering

Dead Loves

just when I thought
I held cowboy & Indian love in
my arms clinging to vanishing hopes

long distant calls summon
rain drops reflected in
a rear-view mirror staring back at me

exposed skeletons I carry
& drag myself bent
into four worlds that love me
& hate me for who I am

yet all I wanted was the same as what I gave

trapped is not the word
that lets my pen cry dry tears
as I walk proudly on the rez
cherishing every dead love

I have kept alive

Cowboys & Indians

I washed my feet
with holy water,
slipped into Justins,
reached for black felt
& covered the night

it does not change
those moments
while they lasted
but it hardens the heart even more
on the ride home

you always knew that
eight was a magic number
for cowboys
& that a flying V
symbolizes ownership

what you didn't know
was that cowboys & Indians
are the same

Narrow Sympathies

narrow sympathies
black with numbers
leading to ten
little Indians & beyond
guide my quivering fingers
to the livewire

dialing was the easy part
& a formality expected
but the coiled fist wasn't
squeezing the damp receiver
pulsating blood-thrust temper
when the straight words were spoken
without contempt

"I don't love you enough to hate to you"

the heart already knew the loss
now call someone new

Shower Songs

numbing lonesomeness
with a quick-easy orgasm
is not about sexual freedom,
grand declarations,
or noisy cowboys

this Indian has never won
the lottery or found clever analogies
that keeps my picture
sitting on your desk at work

it never occurred to me
that life is something to hide
like black gossip,
bad shower songs,
or bulging body implants

relationships cannot be played out
in clubs,
cliques,
or over the internet

bravery opens the mind
& frankly, I'm ready

Icicles & Arrows

I dreamed
a weak Indian man turned
into a hard cowgirl

a secret hungry & gossip full
awakening in the evolution of
the Pipe Carrier's fear
was the terrorist child blossoming into rage
like a murderer's protégé

transforming a jingle-dress dancer's shifting
cones at the climax of the drum & dream,
icicles & arrows swung from the heart

& there was no turning back

Cougars on Elbow Drive

goddesses don't belly lurk
lie still in the capillaries
cocooning butterflies in the stomach
that excite young men looking for
old cougars perched on dead
logs waiting for the young stuff to
strut by in boullettes, muscle shirts and taut pants
so tight you can see the veins in their asses
not to mention the front bulging with cash

tilt your Stetson, cowgirl,

god shows off wranglers now-a-days
cloud-high at the tepee village off McLeod Trail
half an hour before the chuckwagons boom
mud and spit pleasers for the feigner Cher girl watchers
eager to try out O.C.T.s (old cougar tricks)
on guys and gals alike

"how do I know this?" you ask
well, I've never seen Cher (in person that is)
but hunted a few cougars in my time
down by the cool waters a short walk on Elbow Drive

---

cougars: slang for older women who pursue young men

A Cowgirl's Wrath of Words

crawling
out of that head-smashed-in
toothless cowgirl mouth
is volcanic mass
and fiery energy

conceit
spawning
electrical rage,
spitting fire,
erupting a wrath
of words meant
to burn to ash
goodness
smouldering
in fiery chambers

tell me one last time
"this is the end"

Broken Glass

Lacerated
cowboy & Indian
hearts
shatter
love
mingling
in broken glass

Jagged
deadly
sharp
words & edges
stab
knowingly

Warm & salty
blood
passes twisted lips
to kiss historic wounds
reopened to air

& love dies
again

West

my pickup truck left
the bunk house west

a trip still seductive
after years groping
hands smoke illusion
my Dodge Dakota reeks joy

dirty looks
dirty moves
dirty clothes
dirty dances
by the muddy river bank
dig toes deep
into the softness
of the warm mud

hands glide
the smoking engine pumps
iron & smoke
panting giggles
reefer after reefer

A Cowboy Long Gone

cowboys never bawl

they leave behind broken
pieces of themselves
to cover naked space

saying "goodbye"
in the same breath
they leave with

eight seconds of long silence means
a cowboy is long gone

Shadow Walk

Shadow Walk

I look for you everywhere
in the cars that speed past
on my way to and from work

I stare at similar faces sitting
across the room at The Grind
where two cups of cappuccino await

I hang out at Riverside Park
propped at the base of a weeping willow
and watch the Thompson River drift by

I write poetry on dead leaves
that create patterns in the sand
in late September mornings

I argue with the wind's words
about dull death, autumn mornings and moon colours
that outgrow youthful passion

then I shadow walk with lovers

Black Flowers

I captured sunrays
in the palms of my hands
when my soul opened

I turned turquoise time
into yellow dreams
with my eyes closed

I cracked a lightning song
& broke open
the jagged edges of memory

of salt water & black flowers

Stone Prayer

I climb the jagged mountains
weighed down with a black burden
spewing bitter curses
at the tyrant falling
in love with my brothers & sisters

I will lie on its sacred, cool surface
arms overflowing crying colours
fingers cleaving to the Red Rock
that weeps ghostly compassion

for those too young to die
tormenting deaths at the mercy of
the cruel master dangling at
the end of festering needles disguised
as a waiting lover

& when I have scraped off
the last bit of hardened blood from
the hospital floor, disposed the soiled sheets

I will carry your brittle, wilted wreath of skin
clinging racked bones
singing heaven's Good-Bye Song
to the waiting grave once more

then I will look death in the eye
& wait my turn

Blowing Kisses

dim sparks circle a swollen Moon
growing utopian words
escaping ghost walkers
throwing sticks & stones
pleading with Sweetgrass
reaching heaven below Saddle Mountain

the yellow arms of the Moon
give back blowing kisses & ghostly gifts

Joan's Poem

for my sister-in-law, Joan

Earl's on top of Robson Street is crammed
my ravenous soul sees
blood light lines leading and digging
the surgeon's path through
this cowgirl's alleyways and corridors
connecting lung chambers and heart
hiding long-past troubles that brought
her to this plastic stranger in the first place

and in the lounge full
of boom baby boys cheering victory
over the win and loss of the 2005 World Series,
I cannot celebrate their triumphs

I will rejoice in her life though
heavy-hearted I may be
touting nervous giggles of Secwepemc prayer
quietly to myself as trendy and pompous
as those promoting globalisms
in the glint of their eyes

across the table sit
a mob of metrosexual Indian lawyers
promising the fight and retrieval
of the give-away lands Trutch
calculatingly tossed gluttonous settlers . . .

And he waited for the starvation of my sisters — like Joan

The creeks and streams never dry my eyes these days;
through the fog, I see you galloping Chip
full throttle in cloverleaf patterns on the same lands
in the same arenas that brought
our ancestors this far in history

You are so courageous at this moment
I wish I were the heart of a woman — like you.

The Geometry of Cowboys & Indians

distance moves bodies
pinks & browns collide in New Mexico

whirlwinds gulp up dust & stir debris
the desert floor exposes earthquake veins

their love is geometry:
elements at right angles & triangles

hogans are not part of the calculations
unconnected by numbers & words

making nonsense with second-
hand smoke burning eyes

mistake the equation & miscalculate
the empty space as forbidden

Hope

Somewhere in my drive past Hope
my mind travels back to you & I am moved

I imagine clean ocean scents
surrounding you, soft voice whispering
night song to tame this
restless soul

Your touch exploring
the tightness of my body

My heart is taken by you

Two worlds far apart
drifting over emerald-green oceans
of other universes I know
no other will discover

Clean milky waves washing over me
at my arrival on shore's edge

Peacefully I am assured
that those travels to distant planets
are in dreams of Hope
for you — for me

Broken Magic

I am grounded by magic stones
singing red songs

you are filled with beer song
breaking my words

I am white stones
dancing rattle dances

you are flirting with cold words
at closing time

I am black shale
sliding from broken mountain

you are extending empty arms
seeking inert lovers

we are broken magic

Surrender

you can't believe
I am the one
I write about
in the ice words
etched
within my stone poems

I am the sorrel horse
stripped
of its cracked, rotting halter
standing in a freedom field
dumbfounded

I am the early summer snake
shedding its skin
in search of new life
and leaving behind
reminders

I am the lover
who awakens in the mornings
to body imprints, ruffled sheets
and your good notes

I am the one
too lost within myself
to be found in poetry or fields or reminders or beds
or you

all you need to believe
is that I can never surrender

Rain Talk

I stood naked
beneath the shifting grey skies
surrounded by reservation

and spoke of rain that morning
because the drizzle grew
to be a downpour

the night before you also spoke
of rain and told me how it
weighed you down

to the mud beneath your feet
I saw it differently
below my feet

Fine Print

I keep you hidden
in cowboy & Indian poetry

beaded neatly
between & beneath lines

designed precisely
in fine print

I am the keeper
of holy songs & awkward questions

like Koyoti, I shape words into things
forever translucent

Let Go

I remember
I was wild in love
pulling words from my heart,
giving them to Sweetgrass and heaven
below Saddle Mountain

I thought you were there,
in the yellow arms of a swollen moon
where my words blew kisses
& you gave me back
a sacred bundle of undergrowth
as I let go

Surface

I had never known
that another's forest of eyes
could so naturally transform
black tears into pearl snowflakes
falling into night

I had never known that
another's love touch
could turn my body
into shimmering moonlit waves
Grassdancing in the night's moon

I had never known
that another's embrace
could engulf me in
both fury & safety
as the night's moon wafted across the sky
like a Round Dance near dawn

I had never known
that by entering another's body,
the Wildman of Sea & Forest
could drag gentleness & kindness
to the surface of the moon's haze
in the last starlight at daybreak
as if the act were a Red Stone Prayer

I had never known
that another's act of benevolence
was pure & sincere, & that you
could draw my soul
to the surface of daylight

Equinox

wings of Robin
return
to tap prayer
at still dawn

life falls
into rhythmic humming
live electrical wires
carrying
song
through clear sky
& over rippling water

breath murmurs expose
unseen life
passed from man to woman
to child
from winter to spring
from death to life

fragile eggs meet
heatwave motions
silent travel
sailing wings land
on shimmering stems
of dancing green leaves
in spring
Robin is home

Was It You?

Was it you who came back from heaven
galloping in dreamtime on a red-roan star horse
carrying the Higher Power's burden?

The Northern Lights lit a trail to my pithouse.
Its shimmering movement of waves hummed
a universal Horse Dance melody
and the song went like this
tcu'smensten — I came looking for you.

Was it you who came back from heaven
whipping lightning from your bridle reins?
Ts7ek'w ne si'test
exploding the night into dazzling magenta and lime light
like the sun's luminous rays sparkling on Shuswap Lake
in the heart of Secwepemcullulcw — Shuswap country.

Was it you who came back from heaven
looking for the blue soul
searching for the meaning of radiance

ell qwensti'stctn re Tqeltku'kwpi7 e stse7ek'ws —
— and I prayed for a miracle to fall from God's eye.

Was it you who came back from heaven
to bury *Tqeltu' kwupi7* gift in the very centre of my heart?

Ell me7 pelq'i'lc ne tqeltk te tmicw —
— and then leaving to return to the sky?

It was you, wasn't it?

Shape-Shift

undergoing
white & red rhythm

swelling
muscle mass

expanding
raw air of body heat tricks

shape-shifting
like Koyoti's out-of-sight desires

twisting
of tongue & manes tepee

creeping
through sweat

dripping
wet love on silk sheets

yodelling
cowboy grassland's song

giggling
with delight at dawn's

breaking
ochre clouds on sky

screaming
bliss on beautiful black rez

nearing
detonation of cowboy & Indian love

amalgamating
once & for all

ABOUT THE AUTHOR

—

Garry Gottfriedson was born, raised and lives in Kamloops, British Columbia. He is a self-employed rancher with a Masters degree in Education from Simon Fraser University. Gottfriedson was awarded the Gerald Red Elk Creative Writing Scholarship by the Naropa Institute in Boulder, Colorado, where he studied under Allen Ginsberg, Anne Waldman, Marianne Faithful and others. He has read from his work across North America and Europe, and, more recently, in Taiwan. His work has been anthologized and published nationally and internationally. He is the author of *In Honor of Our Grandmothers: Imprints of Cultural Survival* (Theytus Books, 1994); *100 Years of Contact* (Secwepemc Cultural Education Society, 1990); *Glass Tepee,* (Thistledown Press, 2002), nominated for First People's Publishing Award 2004); and *Painted Pony* (Partners in Publishing, 2005), his first children's story. He is presently finishing his first novel.